Previous page: Lydd Graveyard
where Larissa is buried

Grand Duchess Olga

Grand Duchess Tatiana

Grand Duchess Mazie

Grand Duchess Anastasia

Tsarina Alexandra

Tsar Nicholas II

Tsarevich Alexei

NO RESTING PLACE FOR A ROMANOV

No Resting Place for a Romanov

Published and written by
Sue Edwards

Published by Sue Edwards

British Library cataloguing in publication data
A catalogue record of this book is available
from the British Library

Designed by
Andrew McColm of Nicholls McColm
44 Kings Drive, Eastbourne, Sussex BN21 2PB

Printed in Great Britain by
Principal Colour
12 Branbridges Industrial Estate,
East Peckham, Tonbridge, Kent TN12 5HF

ISBN 0 9529292 1 X

'I cannot forecast to you the action of Russia.
It is a riddle wrapped in a mystery inside an enigma'.

Winston Churchill.
1st October 1939.

Contents

Introduction

I came across, quite by chance, the lonely grave of Larissa Feodorovna Tudor whilst researching for my book 'Children of the Weald'. Not knowing Lydd very well I was, in fact, looking in the wrong churchyard for there are two in Lydd - one surrounding the beautiful old church of All Saints' and another about half a mile away owned by the Shepway District Council.

What immediately drew my attention to the grave was the inscription on the headstone which contained the name Feodorovna for I knew that this was only used by female members of the Russian Imperial Family and I was equally puzzled as to how she had married someone with the name of Owen Tudor. For those of us who look back on our history lessons with affection will remember that Owen Tudor was the founder of the Tudor dynasty and it seemed to me that for two people to bear such incongruous names was more than a little odd. Could this be fact or was it someone playing a huge joke!

Over the following months, as I probed deeper into the story, much of what I learned about the couple would so often prove to be contradictory. I would travel along so many blind alleys only to come back to where I had originally started, but in the end with a great deal of help from local people and the Tudor family I was, at last, able to piece together the curious tale of Owen and Larissa Feodorovna Tudor.

It has not been an easy task for unlike most research there are still numerous questions to be asked that can never be answered. Many of the players in the story are now dead and on the death of Colonel Tudor it was found that he had destroyed every single document relating to his life with Larissa.

After several years of dogged determination I have now been able to put together some of the jig-saw. 'No Resting Place For A Romanov' charts the tragic life of two young people whose obvious love for each other was to last no more than three years and poses the question did, at least one member of the Russian Imperial Family finally find peace and contentment, albeit for so short a time, with a young lieutenant in the King's Own Hussars?

CITIES CONNECTED
WITH THE
ROMANOV PLOT

Riga

London

LYDD

Berlin

Paris

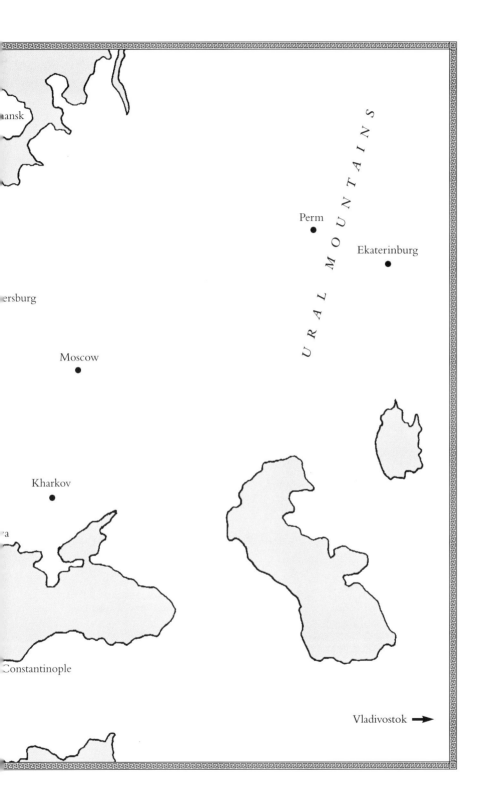

THE FAMILIES OF
TSAR NICHOLAS II
& QUEEN VICTORIA

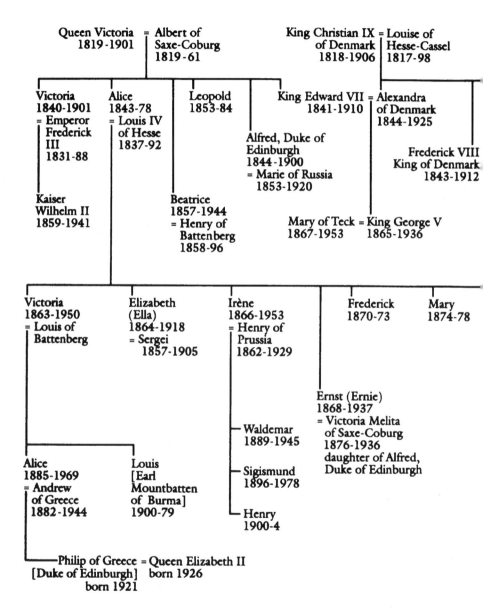

Queen Victoria = Albert of
1819-1901 | Saxe-Coburg
| 1819-61

King Christian IX = Louise of
of Denmark | Hesse-Cassel
1818-1906 | 1817-98

Victoria
1840-1901
= Emperor
Frederick
III
1831-88

Alice
1843-78
= Louis IV
of Hesse
1837-92

Leopold
1853-84

King Edward VII = Alexandra
1841-1910 | of Denmark
| 1844-1925

Alfred, Duke of
Edinburgh
1844-1900
= Marie of Russia
1853-1920

Frederick VIII
King of Denmark
1843-1912

Kaiser
Wilhelm II
1859-1941

Beatrice
1857-1944
= Henry of
Battenberg
1858-96

Mary of Teck = King George V
1867-1953 1865-1936

Victoria
1863-1950
= Louis of
Battenberg

Elizabeth
(Ella)
1864-1918
= Sergei
1857-1905

Irène
1866-1953
= Henry of
Prussia
1862-1929

Frederick
1870-73

Mary
1874-78

Ernst (Ernie)
1868-1937
= Victoria Melita
of Saxe-Coburg
1876-1936
daughter of Alfred,
Duke of Edinburgh

Waldemar
1889-1945

Alice
1885-1969
= Andrew
of Greece
1882-1944

Louis
[Earl
Mountbatten
of Burma]
1900-79

Sigismund
1896-1978

Henry
1900-4

Philip of Greece = Queen Elizabeth II
[Duke of Edinburgh] born 1926
born 1921

12

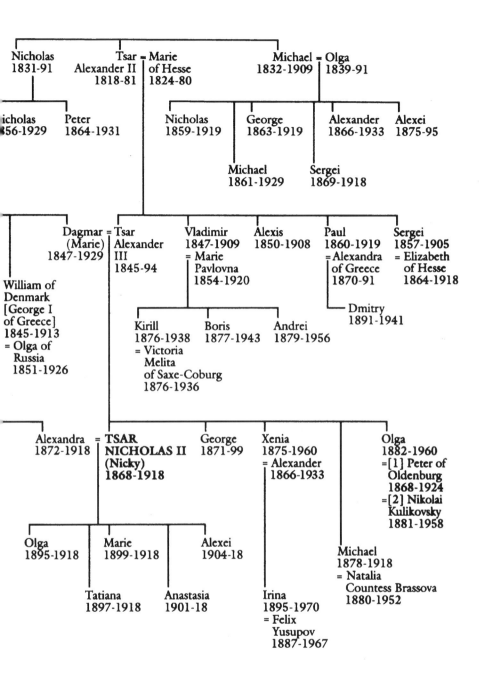

Nicholas
1831-91

Tsar = Marie
Alexander II | of Hesse
1818-81 | 1824-80

Michael = Olga
1832-1909 | 1839-91

icholas
56-1929

Peter
1864-1931

Nicholas
1859-1919

George
1863-1919

Alexander
1866-1933

Alexei
1875-95

Michael
1861-1929

Sergei
1869-1918

Dagmar = Tsar
(Marie) | Alexander
1847-1929 | III
1845-94

Vladimir
1847-1909
= Marie
Pavlovna
1854-1920

Alexis
1850-1908

Paul
1860-1919
= Alexandra
of Greece
1870-91

Sergei
1857-1905
= Elizabeth
of Hesse
1864-1918

William of
Denmark
[George I
of Greece]
1845-1913
= Olga of
Russia
1851-1926

Kirill
1876-1938
= Victoria
Melita
of Saxe-Coburg
1876-1936

Boris
1877-1943

Andrei
1879-1956

Dmitry
1891-1941

Alexandra
1872-1918

= TSAR
NICHOLAS II
(Nicky)
1868-1918

George
1871-99

Xenia
1875-1960
= Alexander
1866-1933

Olga
1882-1960
=[1] Peter of
Oldenburg
1868-1924
=[2] Nikolai
Kulikovsky
1881-1958

Olga
1895-1918

Marie
1899-1918

Alexei
1904-18

Michael
1878-1918
= Natalia
Countess Brassova
1880-1952

Tatiana
1897-1918

Anastasia
1901-18

Irina
1895-1970
= Felix
Yusupov
1887-1967

1

TO
MY VERY BELOVED
LARISSA FEODOROVNA
WHO DIED JULY 18TH 1926
AGED 28 YEARS
THE WIFE OF
OWEN TUDOR
3RD THE KING'S OWN HUSSARS

Tucked away in the corner of a grave yard, in the small marsh-land town of Lydd, is a mysterious and solitary grave. Set well away from the other graves, with only a Cypress tree for company, it is immediately apparent to the passer-by that this is no ordinary grave. An elegant marble tombstone stands at it's head enclosed by ornate iron railings designed and erected by a London firm of Undertakers and Stonemasons, Becketts of Baker Street. This in itself is, perhaps, not worthy of a second glance but it is to the epitaph inscribed on the tombstone that one's attention is instantly drawn for it is so worded seemingly to invite speculation as to the true identity of the person buried there.

Who was this young woman whose life had ended so tragically in only her twenty-eighth year and who was Owen Tudor? Did they ever exist or were their names merely a misnomer in order to hide a more complex explanation.

Larissa's grave

16

"Ferndale", Lydd. The Tudors' house.

Owen and Larissa Tudor were, in fact, remembered quite clearly by some of the town elders. In 1923 as a newly married couple, they had taken up residence in a modest house called "Ferndale" overlooking the Rype (a village green said to be the largest green of its kind in Kent). Owen Tudor had transferred from the King's Own Hussars to the 3rd Battalion, the Royal Tank Corps, which had that year set up camp on the cold and dismal marshland just outside the town and while Owen Tudor was away each day, Larissa, a slim built pretty woman with an abundance of dark curly hair, spent much of her time lying on an invalid bed. Some of the local people remember her arriving in Lydd by train and on that occasion she appeared to be walking quite normally.

The couple lived quietly and Owen Tudor did not seem to socialise with his fellow officers. As a way of earning extra cash much of his spare time was taken up with breaking in horses for the army and for the local farmers at the nearby Tourney Hall stables in Lydd. His extraordinary understanding and control over the animals was to earn him the respect of the local farmers who would often spend hours watching as he painstakingly coaxed a horse into final submission. He was also Master of the Tank Corps Basset Hounds and during the hunting season would ride out, duties permitting, every Tuesday and Friday.

Owen Tudor was also quite a hit with the local ladies who all agreed that he was the most handsome young man they had ever set eyes upon and one can only speculate as to how many female hearts missed a beat or two when the young lieutenant rode by each day on his fine horse. Sadly, although always cordial towards them, Larissa his beautiful wife had already captured his heart.

"Ferndale", facing the Rype.

"Tourney Hall", The Bass family stands in the foreground.

Confined to the house as she was, Larissa quickly became an enigma to the towns people and it was not long before rumour and myth began to circulate around this small community. "Larissa was a belly-dancer from Constantinople", "Larissa was a Russian Princess" and worst of all "Larissa was a Turkish whore". The fact that, as a couple, the Tudors kept to themselves and because Larissa was known to speak with just the hint of a foreign accent only gave more credence to these outlandish stories. Though the year was 1923 and five years after the cessation of the First World War, small rural towns often had little contact with the outside world and in particular Lydd, lying as it does on the southern most part of the Romney Marshes, had because of its very isolation, evolved into a community of fiercely independent 'marsh dwellers'. It is, therefore, not surprising that the locals were generally suspicious of anyone who did not fit into the natural 'pecking order' of society - no one realised at the time that Larissa was slowly dying from a wasting disease known as 'Spinal Caries' - a condition that would very soon cause her death.

'Spinal Caries' is loosely known as a bone crumbling disease which attacks the vertebrae causing it to gradually disintegrate. In the early 20's without the benefits of today's medical knowledge, this disease could often be brought on by a severe fall and as it took hold of the body, Tuberculosis would set in eventually causing death to the victim. Larissa contracted Tuberculosis in 1924.

Owen Frederick Morton Tudor was born into a Naval family on the 21st October, 1900. His father and uncle were both distinguished admirals and it was naturally expected that the young

Midshipman Owen Frederick Morton Tudor

Owen would follow them into the Royal Navy. After serving for a year as a midshipman aboard the HMS Repulse he was forced to leave the navy because of poor eyesight and on the 21st October, 1919 he was commissioned as a Second Lieutenant in the 20th Hussars. Whilst at the Royal Military Academy, Sandhurst, he won the coveted 'Saddle' and was obviously destined for a brilliant career in one of the cavalry regiments.

He was also an outstanding athlete and had from an early age excelled at sport – in 1919 and 1920 he was awarded the prestigious Victor Ludorum. From 1924 to 1926 he represented the Royal Tank Corps mainly in track events, some taking place at the nearby Shorncliffe Barracks in Folkestone. In 1926 he was selected to represent England in the 120 yards hurdle and in that year successfully competed in the Kent County

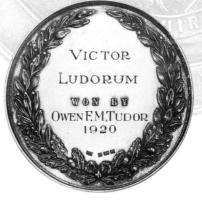

Sporting Prize Medals won by Owen Tudor at the Royal Military Academy Sandhurst.

Lt. Owen Frederick Morton Tudor

Championship both for long jump and the 480 yards relay. He also played polo, hockey and rugby to a high degree of proficiency. In army parlance he was a 'good all rounder' whose sporting prowess must surely have been viewed as a prize catch by the regiment.

After a short spell with the 20th Hussars he was, on the 23rd November, 1921, transferred to the 3rd The King's Own Hussars and very quickly posted to Constantinople where he remained until 1923.

2

Town Square, Lydd c.1920's

How he came to meet Larissa is not known. Many conflicting stories have been written on the subject but there is not one shred on evidence to support any of these 'theories'. Documents that might have shed some light on the matter have either mysteriously disappeared or have been deliberately destroyed. Whatever the true facts are, it is unthinkable that Owen Tudor on the brink of such a promising career, would take up with and eventually marry a Turkish belly dancer or a Turkish lady of 'ill-repute' more especially as he was well under the permitted age for marriage by a serving officer. (In 1923 army regulations expressly forbade officers to marry until they were 30 years of age when they would become eligible for the usual allowances and army quarters – in certain circumstances permission might be granted by the Commanding Officer but only if the young man was of independent means). As Owen Tudor was known to have no private income permission would have automatically been withheld and particularly in view of Larissa's alleged 'professional activities'!

It is possible that the couple met in Constantinople but why the young lieutenant should rush the ailing Larissa back home to marry is a question many historians have pondered over. Aged 22 years, with no private income how did Owen Tudor hope to maintain a sick wife on his meagre salary without the benefits that would have come to him had he obtained the consent of his Commanding Officer? What had prompted this young man to marry a chronic invalid when, presumably, he could have had the pick of any young woman from his own class? Somewhere hidden in the maze of conflicting evidence surrounding this couple an explanation of the truth must surely lie for so many facts simply do not add up.

Nothing is known of Larissa's background. The Tudors' Marriage Certificate, which might well have held some sort of clue, merely shows that her maiden name was Haouk and that she was the daughter of Adolph Haouk a conveniently deceased man of 'independent means'. The marriage took place at the St. George's Register Office, Hanover Square in London on the 16th of August, 1923 with a K. M. Huntingdon and a D. Swinburne acting as witnesses. (The identity of K. M. Huntingdon is not known but his name appears again as a witness on Owen Tudor's marriage to his second wife - Denis Swinburne was a first cousin, by marriage, to Owen Tudor). Larissa's age was given as 27 years old (a good 5 years older than her husband) and her attested signature to the Marriage Certificate is recorded as plain 'L. Haouk'.

Right from the beginning of their married life much of what we know about them is so often at variance with documented data.

Lydd High Street c.1920's

Larissa's age on the Marriage Certificate is shown as 27 years old although some 3 years later her Death Certificate states that she was 29 years old – on her tombstone it is clearly marked that she died at the age of 28 years. (This type of discrepancy was not at all uncommon in those days as any Registrar of Births, Deaths and Marriages will readily confirm) but in the case of Owen Tudor, a well educated man who presumably supervised the funeral arrangements, it is unlikely that he would not have detected so many obvious mistakes.

On the Marriage Certificate, Larissa is referred to as 'Larissa Haouk', as is her attested signature, but on her Death Certificate, Letters of Administration and headstone the name Feodorovna is mysteriously included.

Owen Tudor's profession on the Marriage Certificate is given 'as of independent means' a fact which his immediate family strongly refute. His army rank on the Death Certificate and Letters of Administration is attested as 'Lieutenant of the 3rd Battalion the Royal Tank Corps' and yet on Larissa's headstone he is referred to 'as of the 3rd the King's Own Hussars'. Clearly far too many intrinsically incompatible statements thus far to go under the heading of clerical errors!

Larissa, for some reason, had thought it expedient not to make a last Will and Testament although her estate, when she died, was worth £227.4s. 5d. (Two hundred and twenty seven pounds, four shillings and five pence). By today's standards this would seem to be a small sum of money but one has to remember that in the year 1926 this sum represented the cost of a fair sized house. Just how did a 'Turkish lady of ill-repute' acquire so

All Saints church, Lydd

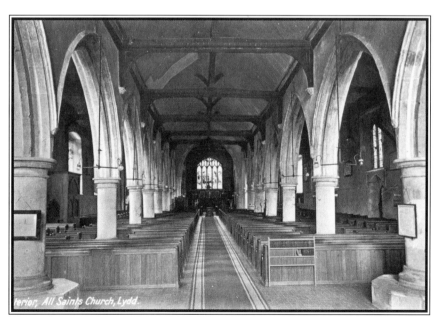

Interior, All Saints Church, Lydd

much money – certainly not from her alleged activities and most certainly not from her impoverished husband!

Was she simply too ill to execute any kind of document or was this just another deliberate move on the part of the Tudors to conceal their identity for it has often been suggested that Larissa refrained from making a Will fearing that, at some time in the future, her signature could be made available for public scrutiny? This argument, however, must be discounted for she had already put her signature to a document – her Marriage Certificate!

Larissa's actual signature taken from her wedding certificate

Right: Owen and Larissa's marriage certificate.

Crown copyright: Published by permission of the Controller of H.M.S.O. and Office for National Statistics.

Marriage solemnized at _the Register Office_ in the District of _St. George Hanover Square_ in the County of _London_

No.	When Married.	Name and Surname.	Age.	Condition.	Rank or Profession.	Residence at the time of Marriage.	Father's Name and Surname.	Rank or Profession of Father.
24	192 3	Gwen Frederick Wixon Vixian	22 years	Bachelor	of Independent means	York Hotel Mayfair	Henry Wixon Vixian	of Independent means
August 1923	Farina Haouk	27 years	Spinster	—	York Hotel Mayfair	Adolph Haouk (deceased)	of Independent means

Married in the _Register Office_ according to the Rites and Ceremonies of the _————_ by me,

This Marriage was solemnized between us, {
G. F. W. Vixian
L. Haouk
} in the Presence of us, {
R. H. Hamilton
R. Livingstone
} Harry A Hamilton

N. T. Ashley Registrar
G. Livingstone Superintendent Registrar

CERTIFIED to be a true copy of an entry in the certified copy of a register of Marriages in the Registration District of _St. George Hanover Square_

Given at the GENERAL REGISTER OFFICE, under the Seal of the said Office, the 17th day of August 19 93

MX 677106

Form A513MX

Dd 8425619 100M 6/93 Mcr2342610

31

CERTIFIED COPY OF AN ENTRY OF DEATH

GIVEN AT THE GENERAL REGISTER OFFICE

Application Number. R007186.

REGISTRATION DISTRICT Romney Marsh

1986 DEATH in the Sub-district of Lydd in the County of Kent

No.	When and where died	Name and surname	Sex	Age	Occupation	Cause of death	Signature, description and residence of informant	When registered	Signature of registrar
Columns:—	1	2	3	4	5	6	7	8	9
918	Eighteenth July 1986 Ferndale Lydd Kent	Larissa Leoterina Lydia Ludor	Female	29 years	Wife of Edward Leonard Ludor Merchant Seaman	1 Spinal Cord Injuries Molenvag Islander	O.F.N. Ludor Husband Widow J Decent Present at the Death 4th August Ferndale, Lydd Rept Inst July a Post E.A	1986	Y.Michell Registrar

CERTIFIED to be a true copy of an entry in the certified copy of a Register of Deaths in the District above mentioned.

Given at the GENERAL REGISTER OFFICE, under the Seal of the said Office, the 6th day of August 19 93.

DXZ 144285

See note overleaf

CAUTION:- It is an offence to falsify a certificate or to make or knowingly use a false certificate or a copy of a false certificate intending it to be accepted as genuine to the prejudice of any person or to possess a certificate knowing it to be false without lawful authority.

Administration.

DEATH ON OR AFTER 1st JANUARY, 1898.

BE IT KNOWN that *Larissa Feodorovna Tudor of Ferndale - Lydd in the County of Kent*

died *there* on the *18th* day of *July* 19 *26*

intestate

AND BE IT FURTHER KNOWN that at the date hereunder written Letters of Administration of all the Estate which by law devolves to and vests in the personal representative of the intestate were granted by His Majesty's High Court of Justice at the Principal Probate Registry thereof to

Owen Frederick Morton Tudor of The Royal Tank Corps Barracks - Lydd aforesaid - a Lieutenant in Hm. Army - the lawful husband -

of the said intestate.

Dated the *2nd.* day of *October* 192 *6.*

Gross value of Estate ...... £ *227 - 4 - 5*

~~Net value of Personal Estate £~~

8606 5097F/48(B) 9,000 6/35 146 F & S

Left: Death Certificate. Above: Letter of administration

The windswept beaches of Lydd

The Russ

Standing left to right: Grand Duchess Mari
Tsar Nicholas II, Grand Duchess A

rial Family

a. Seated left to right: Grand Duchess Olga,
revich Alexei, Grand Duchess Tatiana

A life-time resident of Lydd, Mr. Herbert Prebble, now well into his 90's, clearly remembers Owen Tudor riding his horse to work each day which he stabled at a farm just behind their home on the Rype. He said that Owen Tudor was a 'perfect gentleman' who always found time to acknowledge Mr. Prebble should their paths ever cross and he commented that no expense seemed to be spared on the upkeep of the animal. Owen Tudor would also frequently stop for any of the local children while they made a fuss of the animal. Mr. Prebble's memory of Larissa was not so clear, however, as he only caught the occasional glimpse of her in the garden but he stressed, in the strongest possible terms, that she was indeed a very beautiful woman and he spoke of her 'as that Russian Princess'.

So far, what we know about this couple intrigues rather than answers the many conflicting stories. For example, the term 'Russian princess' and the sudden use of the name Feodorovna begins to excite the imagination and in order to separate myth from reality it is necessary to search for proof of their authenticity.

Little importance should be attached to the title of 'Russian princess' for at the time of the Russian Revolution many aristocrats escaped from the terrible civil uprisings to live out their lives in rural parts of England frequently claiming, rightly or wrongly, to be closely related to the Tsar. It is not surprising, therefore, that these emigres, often possessing unpronounceable names and speaking in a strange tongue, should be referred to as Russian 'princes or princesses'. Larissa was often given that title by the people of Lydd with little thought being given to the rumour that she was originally supposed to have come from Turkey!

The name Feodorovna is one closely associated with the Romanovs. Used in the context of a patronymn it is a title adopted by the women who marry descendants of the Tsars. For example, Tsar Alexander II (1818-81) married Princess Marie (Maria Feodorovna) of Hesse and by Rhine (1824-80) – Tsar Alexander III (1845-94) married Princess Dagmar (Marie Feodorovna) of Denmark (1847-1928) and the last Tsar, Nicholas II (1868-1918) married Princess Alexandra (Alexandra Feodorovna) of Hesse and by Rhine (1872-1918). Grand Duke Sergei Alexandrovitch (1857-1905), a direct descendant of Tsar Nicholas I, married Princess Elizabeth (Elizabeth Feodorovna) of Hesse and by Rhine (1864-1918).

It seems unlikely that the sudden inclusion of the name Feodorovna by Owen Tudor on Larissa's Death Certificate, her Letters of Administration and on the tombstone would have been merely the result of a moments madness on the part of a distraught husband for this simply was not Owen Tudor's style. His conduct throughout the whole affair was nothing short of exemplary and until the day he died he never talked about their life together. Was there a reason for Owen Tudor's reticence – some awful secret he had pledged to carry to his grave – a secret so dire that should it ever be revealed he and his family could well perish at the hands of a silent enemy?

Although this explanation may appear to be capricious – almost bordering on the fantasy world of 'cloak and dagger', when allied to the rumours concerning Larissa's true identity it then becomes more than just a possibility.

During the night of the 16th July, 1918, in the basement room of a house in Ekaterinburg, the entire Russian Imperial Family were systematically slaughtered, all in the space of 20 minutes – a dynasty was finished forever in a room measuring no more than 16 ft x 14 ft – a loving and closely-knit family brutally murdered.

4

Grand Duchess Tatiana

Much has been written about the tragic events of that terrible day using information supplied by dubious sources. No one will ever know, for certain, what really did happen but when reports of the murder began to slowly filter through to the outside world it was generally thought that England, and in particular, the British Royal Family could have prevented the tragedy by offering asylum to the Tsar and his family.

Secret negotiations had, in fact, been going on between members of the British Government, the new provisional Revolutionary Government and King George V right from the beginning of the Imperial Family's captivity but, as is so often the way, nothing was done until it was too late.

To the Prime Minister of the day, David Lloyd George, this was welcome news for he had always been against the idea of asylum sensing that the huge expense of maintaining the Imperial Family in England would not find favour with the electorate. To King George V and his mother, Queen Alexandra, both closely related to the Tsar and Tsarina, this course of action was to haunt them for the rest of their lives.

In a last ditch attempt to rescue the remaining relatives of the Tsar, a British battleship, the HMS Marlborough, was dispatched to Yalta where it picked up Marie Feodorovna, Dowager Emperess of Russia, (the Tsar's mother), her entourage and many Russian nobles. With it's huge load of emigres, the HMS Marlborough set sail for Malta and freedom thus enabling many of the emigres to safely settle in countries around the world. The Dowager Empress returned to her native Denmark and until the day she died refused to believe that her beloved family were dead.

The bodies of the Russian Imperial Family were quickly disposed of leaving no clues as to their final resting place and in the aftermath bizarre stories began to circulate. "The Tsar had, after all, escaped" - "The Russian Imperial Family were living in America" - "They had been sighted in France, England and Denmark"! Various 'children' of the Tsar were rumoured to have fled from the shootings and would, in fact, over a period of many years, lay claim to the Russian Imperial throne. It was not until the 20th century that these claims would finally be disproved.

In 1991, close to the Ekaterinburg/Perm railway line, which runs directly through the Ural mountains, fragmented bones of the Russian Royal Family and their attendants were exhumed. In all, nine skeletons were pieced together and after extensive DNA testing it was proved conclusively that five of the bodies belonged to the Imperial Family. Alexei, the Tsar's son and one daughter were found to be missing.

Those responsible for the testing of the bones could not agree among themselves as to whether the missing daughter was the Grand Duchess Tatiana or the Grand Duchess Anastasia although some of the scientists were of the opinion that the two missing bodies had been burned prior to the disposal of the rest of the family.

The story of the late Anna Anderson is well documented and recent DNA testing on tissue taken from her body has proved, beyond all doubt, that she was not the Grand Duchess Anastasia

King George V

Queen Alexandra

after all – much to the disbelief of a great number of people who had always supported her claim. For so many years she had given hope to the world that, perhaps, one member of the Russian Imperial Family had, after all, managed to survive the bloody massacre in Ekaterinburg. Was it possible that Larissa Tudor's lonely grave in England held a key to the mystery?

5

Emblem of the Royal Tank Corps

Without doubt Owen and Larissa Tudor had something to hide. Their reclusive lifestyle and the fact that they lived in a small unprepossessing house was not, in those days, the usual way of life for a serving officer and his wife. Certainly Owen Tudor would have very little time to socialise for not only had he a sick invalid to care for but his active participation in so many sporting activities and his day to day job with Tank Regiment would have taken up a great deal of his time.

The wives of fellow officers should, as a matter of course, have called on Larissa which was the normal way of army etiquette but this we know did not happen and the question must be asked were they deliberately kept away or did they simply not call because of Larissa's so called reputation!

No satisfactory explanation has ever been given as to why Owen Tudor suddenly transferred from the prestigious King's Own Hussars to the Tank Regiment and why, of all places, he should choose to live in the desolate and windswept town of Lydd where winters can be very harsh and the temperature, at best, cold and damp. Even on summer nights the air is bitter – the locals call it 'hand-cold' – so it is hardly the most congenial of places to take a dying woman.

This quiet marshland town, where for a brief moment in time, gave it's name to the invention of a high powered explosive which when tested on the nearby military ranges caused the 'turn of the century' topographer, Walter Jerrold, to write "that Lyddite this powerful explosive has produced all the effects of an earth-quake for many miles around" had by the time of the Tudors' arrival returned to normality. As far as they were

concerned the one thing going for Lydd was its close prox-
imity to the ports of Dover and Folkestone and a daily train to
London providing a quick escape route should the need ever
arise. Was this the reason they chose to live there?

Entrance to Lydd Camp c.1925

Headquaters 3rd. Battalion Royal Tank Corps, Lydd c.1925

Lydd Camp c.1925

Lydd Camp c.1925

3rd Battalion Royal Tank Corps c.1920's

3rd Battalion Royal Tank Corps, procession through Lydd on Carnival Day

3rd Battalion Royal Tank Corps, procession through Lydd on Carnival Day

3rd Battalion Royal Tank Corps, procession through Lydd on Carnival Day

*3rd Battalion Royal Tank Corps
Church Parade through Lydd
High Street c.1925*

Left: Owen Tudor's second wife, bearing a strong resemblance to the Grand Duchess Tatiana, pictured right

The possibility of Larissa being a member of the Russian Imperial Family is further strengthened by the discovery of an entry in a Diary now housed in the Rhodes Library, Oxford.

The late Colonel Richard Meinertzhagen, CBE, DSO, to whom the diary belonged, was a typical English eccentric. Regarded by some as a charlatan or by others as a man wearing many different hats, he had combined the talents of a respected Ornithologist, a secret Agent and distinguished soldier over a period of many years. In 1918, he was employed at the War Office were much of his work involved organising an intelligence service devoted to the happenings in Russia and in that capacity allegedly visited King George V at Buckingham Palace on a weekly basis. It was at one of these meetings that the King asked if anything could be done to rescue the Imperial Russian Family to whom he was very devoted. Colonel Richard Meinertzhagen records in his diary that he offered to look into the possibility of getting some of them out by aircraft but pointed out that it was taking a great risk as failure could result in the murder of the whole family. Eventually on July 1st a plane was sent out to Ekaterinburg but, according to the diary, only one female child was actually rescued. Literally thrown into the waiting aircraft she sustained much bruising but was successfully brought back to England where she supposedly remained. As a footnote, Colonel Meinertzhagen adds that if her identity were known she would be tracked down and murdered as the heir to the Russian throne. The full diary entry, indexed 'Russia: attempt to rescue the Tsar and his family' was written on the 18th August, 1918 prior to Colonel Meinertzhagen leaving for France to take up a position as one of Earl Haig's staff officers.

Colonel Richard Meinertzhagen, CBE, DSO

To describe an event of such importance, that by implication could well have changed the course of history, in a style of almost casual indifference and so phrased that at first one could be forgiven for dismissing the entry as merely the ramblings of a 'romantic dreamer' may well have been intentional on the part of Colonel Meinertzhagen. Could it have been written in such a way as to deliberately mislead and confuse in order to hide the actual truth?

The entry was written exactly one month to the day following the murder of the Russian Imperial Family. One recent development in the Meinertzhagen saga, which could well strengthen the validity of his story, came to light on Friday, the 6th May 1994. In an article printed in one of the leading tabloids he was branded as a fraud and a hoaxer in respect of his ornithological activities. Under the heading 'Birdman's legend is dead as a Dodo', Meinertzhagen is accused of suppling the Natural History Museum with specimen birds which he had not caught himself but had 'borrowed' from other museums - restuffed them - and then passed them off as his own. Leading ornithologists were scathing in their comments about his integrity - they accused him of forging many of the birds' labels and of lying about how he had found them. He was given the CBE in recognition of his work in this field although he was

Right: Owen Tudor's second wife
Opposite page:
Grand Duchess Tatiana

suspected of having duped the establishment and for this he was never forgiven.

However, on Wednesday, the 31st of December, 1997 another article appeared in the same newspaper claiming that perhaps Meinertzhagen may have been telling the truth after all. One

particular bird, a Forest Owlet, which he had always maintained was found while trekking in a remote part of India (a claim that was never believed) has now been found in that area by two American scientists. This must, at the very least, give some credence to Meinertzhagen's story.

We will never know for sure but possibly in the future, when more secret files are opened up to the General Public, an answer will be found - just like the recent siting of the Forest Owlet!

7

Grand Duchess Anastasia

If Colonel Meinertzhagen's diary entry is to be believed, was there a connection between the alleged rescue of one of the Tsar's children and the reclusive Larissa Feodorovna Tudor living in Lydd? Particular attention should be paid to the last few lines where it refers to a child being literally thrown into a waiting aircraft, much bruised, for it could be said that such rough handling of a delicate young woman may well have resulted in her suffering from Spinal Caries, the same disease that caused Larissa's death.

Colonel Meinertzhagen's son, Richard, readily admits that in recent years his father's exploits have received a bad press but as he was careful to point out, after personally researching many of the stories, he had found them to be quite true! With regard to the attempted rescue plan, this he would neither confirm or deny that it had ever taken place for there was simply no documentation to support his father's claim.

What of the intervening years between 1918 and 1923 when our story begins? It has been suggested that the alleged rescue did not go quite according to plan and that the pilot of the plane was forced to fly direct to Vladivostok instead of stopping to re-fuel at prearranged fuel dumps along the flight path. An ordeal in itself, for a terrified and sick young girl who had then to endure another long haul to the safety of Japanese waters where she was supposedly put under the protection of Prince Arthur of Connaught (Uncle to King George V) who was at the time visiting the country on a goodwill mission. Still under his protection she is thought to have been smuggled on board a ship bound for Canada and thence to England and anonymity.

Could it have really happened like this or was it just the fanciful dreams of a man known to revel in the 'derring do's' of life? From 1918 to 1923 the girl may well have been sheltered in 'safe houses' across the country until such times as her true identity could be erased for ever. What better way than to marry her off to a young subaltern serving in the British Army and arrange for them both to live in a remote part of England. The last sentence of Colonel Meinertzhagen's diary entry warns of the terrible consequences should she ever be discovered.

If, indeed, Larissa Feodorovna Tudor, was a daughter of the last Tsar - which daughter was she? The Grand Duchess Tatiana (second daughter of the Tsar and Tsarina) was born in 1897 - the Grand Duchess Anastasia (their fourth child) was born in 1901. Tatiana must, therefore, be a strong possibility for she and Larissa were practically of the same age and to add another twist to the tale, Larissa's death is registered in London under the name of Larissa T. Tudor! It is difficult to believe that Owen Tudor would yet again brush aside another 'clerical error'.

It matters little today whether Larissa was really a daughter of the last Tsar of Russia or not, for so much has happened in that country since 1918. It would be impossible for the Romanov dynasty to ever govern again and in any case if Larissa was, in truth, the Grand Duchess Tatiana, the Tudors had no children to continue the Romanov line.

It could be said that their life together, if nothing else, was one of the great love stories of the time, for it was a fact that Owen Tudor loved his sick wife very much. Passers-by who sometimes caught a glimpse of Owen and Larissa together outside their home laughing and talking, completely oblivious to the world, as he carried her in his arms across to the Rype on a summers day would ever doubt as much.

What streak of fate brought this young couple together in the first place and why they fell in love will always remain a mystery for although Owen Tudor remarried several years later, he continued to visit Larissa's grave until ill health prevented him from doing so. As a final gesture to his beloved Larissa he placed a beautiful spray of yellow silk Chrysanthemums on her grave where they remained until 1995, a defiant and somewhat faded declaration of their love for each other.

8

Owen Tudor

On the 29th January, 1927, Owen Tudor, surprisingly, rejoined his old regiment, the 3rd The King's Own Hussars, which must immediately pose the question was he simply 'loaned' to the Tank Regiment in order to hide a secret known only to a few. His unauthorised marriage to a lady of 'ill repute' would, in the normal way, have brought disgrace on the regiment and his army career finished for good, but no such obstacle seemed to stand in his way. On his return to the regiment he was promoted to the rank of captain and retired in 1950 as a lieutenant-colonel. He died at the age of 86 years, in Kent, on the 22nd August, 1987.

Was there another interested person watching over the couple paying for all Larissa's expensive medical care and who, at the end of the day, could instruct a London firm of Undertakers and Stonemasons to erect a very grand memorial decorated throughout with the emblem of the Tudor rose for it is obvious that Owen Tudor's army pay would not cover all those enormous bills?

One final twist to this curious tale is that in the 1920's it was the custom for the base and sides of a grave to bricked with edges of three-course bricks. A builder in Lydd employed by local Undertakers to carry out this work was present in the cemetery at the same time as Larissa's grave was being prepared. When he enquired if his services would be needed for her grave he was told that as she was a Russian princess the usual brickwork would not be required for she was to be buried according to the religious rites of her country.

To end this speculation that has for so long surrounded this enigmatic couple is easily redressed because an explanation must surely lie deep within Larissa's grave. Exhumation of her remains for DNA testing would reveal whether or not she was the Grand Duchess Tatiana and if they proved to be conclusive it would be a humanitarian act to reunite her with her beloved family, for the little town of Lydd is surely no resting place for a Romanov.

Handwriting experts could be asked to compare the two signatures of Tatiana and Larissa and if, in the final analysis, Larissa was found to be just an ordinary girl who had merely captured the heart of a handsome young lieutenant she could, at least, be left in peace in her lonely grave to forever dream her dreams of what might have been.

———————

"Sleep on, my Love, in thy cold bed,
Never to be disquieted!
My last good night! Though wilt not wake;
Till I thy fate shall overtake;
Till age, or grief, or sickness must
Marry thy body to that dust
It so much loves; and fill the room
My heart keeps empty in thy tomb".

Bishop Henry King - 1592-1669

Addenda

Since completing "No Resting Place For a Romanov" a further twist to the tale has suddenly come to light. On the morning of Thursday the 30th July, 1998, it was found that the railings surrounding Larissa's grave had been removed and once again, just like all those years ago, rumour and myth began to circulate around the little town of Lydd.

'Was it the Russian Embassy?' – 'Could it have been the work of grave robbers?' – 'Was it a member of the Romanov family preparing Larissa's body for exhumation?'

Enquiries were made of the Shepway District Council and of the Tudor family but all to no avail for they were just as mystified as the people of Lydd. Then a firm of stone masons arrived at the grave side to clean the headstone and marble surrounds – but on whose orders? As the plot thickened the motive behind all this work was questioned and some distress was caused to the Tudor family for not having been consulted.

Whatever the outcome to this story it is more than just coincidence that this should all happen in the same month as the burial of the Tsar and his family in St. Petersburg and it is a sad fact that Larissa's grave, after so many years, will perhaps become a target for vandalism now that it stands out from all the other graves.

Somehow the romance and mystique has died for it was a special grave whose quiet dignity lay in it's faded elegance.

Larissa's grave with railings   *After railings were removed*

"Having belatedly realized the danger to which his cousins were now exposed he (George V) may have instigated or at least encouraged the British Secret Service to rescue them by bribery or force....

All this is mere conjecture. no evidence exists to link the King with those abortive plans known to have been made by Russians refugees for the rescue of their ex-ruler. Yet it is significant that the Royal Archives at Windsor contain hardly any documents dealing with the imprisonment of the Imperial Russian Family between April 1917 and May 1918, precisely those months during which rescue must have been considered if not planned. The absence of such papers points less to the abandonment of the Tsar by the King than to an exceptional need for secrecy".

Kenneth Rose's biography of King George V

"The exact fate of the Tsar and the Imperial Russian Family remains a mystery".

A History of the Russian Secret Service by Richard Deacon

Bibliography

A Lifelong Passion, by Ardrei Maylunas and Sergei Mironenko

For My Grandchildren, by HRH Princess Alice (Countess of Athlone VA, GCVO, GBE, D.Litt, LL.D).

George the Fifth, (His Life and Reign) by Harold Nicholson

Lydd Museum

Nicholas 11(The Last of the Tsars), by Marco Ferro

Nicholas 11 (The letters of the Tsar to the Tsarina), by John Lane

Nicholas and Alexandra (The Family Album), by Prince Michael of Greece

Nicholas and Alexandra, by Robert K. Massie

Richard Meinertzhagen (Soldier, Scientist and Spy), by Mark Cocker

Royal Russia, by Carol Townend

The File on the Tsar, by Anthony Summers and Tom Mangold

The Hunt for the Tsar, by Guy Richards

The Last Days of the Romanovs, by Robert Wilton

The Lost Fortunes of the Tsars, by William Clarke

The Romanovs (The Final Chapter), by Robert K. Massie

The Royal Victorians, by Denis Judd

The Russian Revolution, by R. Pipes

Acknowledgments

The towns people of Lydd have for so many years protected Larissa's grave and I have dedicated this book to them by way of a small 'thank you'.

I would like to thank the family of Owen Tudor who have been so generous in their support of this book.

I would like to thank Mr. Edward Carpenter, local historian and author of many books on the area around Romney Marsh, who gave me so much of his valuable time and allowed me to reproduce many of his photographs.

Also my thanks to the indefatigable Mrs. Bird and to the family of the late Mr. Herbert Prebble.

A special thanks to my daughter Royanne who, despite struggling with some of the Russian names, successfully transferred my text on to the dreaded 'Floppy Disc'.

My thanks to my son-in-law, Andy McColm, for his design work.

My thanks to my friend Heather Hill for help with the indexing.

My thanks to my son Jonathan, who helped me with my search in the various Record offices

My thanks to Martin Darby of Principal Colour, East Peckham, for the production of this book.

Finally, my thanks to my husband who, over the last four years, gave up so much of his spare time to locate and photograph much of the material contained in the book and for his encouragement and support.

Acknowledgments

Michael Ansell, MA (Forensic Consultant)

Business Archives Council

Hulton Getty Collection

Kensington Palace

Office of Population Census and Surveys

Shorncliffe Garrison, Folkestone

Solo Syndication

The City of Wesminster Council

The Daily Mail

The Mail on Sunday

The Royal Commission on Historical Manuscripts

The Royal Military Academy, Sandhurst

The Sandhurst Library

Ton Hire, Paddock Wood

Wizz Graphics

Illustrations

Illustrations

All extracts, illustrations and photographs etc., have been sourced in good faith with, where possible, the permission of the author, artist, photographer and publisher but in certain circumstances the origins are unknown.

The inclusion of such material is of the utmost importance to students of local history and for it's use I am truly grateful.

Sue Edwards

Index